This book is dedicated to all who find Nature not an adversary to conquer and destroy, but a storehouse of infinite knowledge and experience linking man to all things past and present. They know conserving the natural environment is essential to our future well-being.

OLYMPIC
THE STORY BEHIND THE SCENERY®

by Henry C. Warren

Henry "Hank" Warren holds a degree in zoology from the University of California plus additional course work in ecology. During his National Park Service career, he has served as a naturalist in several national parks. Hank's many years at Olympic National Park have qualified him to narrate the story of this hauntingly beautiful, incredibly lush, and varied national treasure.

Olympic National Park, located in northwestern Washington, was established in 1938 to preserve primeval forests, native Roosevelt elk, outstanding mountainous country, and rugged coastline.

Front cover: Mount Olympus beyond the clouds. Photo by Kirkendall/Spring. Inside front cover: Seastacks along the coast, photo by David Muench. Page 1: Bald eagle in flight, photo by Mark Newman/Animals Animals. Pages 2/3: Mount Olympus at sunset, photo by Ed Cooper.

Edited by Peter C. Howorth. Book design by K. C. DenDooven.

Eighth Printing, 2010 • New Version

Glacier-capped mountains, deep valleys, lush meadows, sparkling lakes, giant trees, unspoiled ocean beaches, teeming

wildlife and the most spectacular temperate rain forest in the
world — this is Olympic National Park, a truly great wilderness.

The Olympic Story

The Olympic Peninsula, dominated by tortuous terrain and surrounded on three sides by water, has stood in isolation for millennia. As eons passed, it developed its own special character preserved today in the park. Often moody, sometimes unforgiving, it nevertheless captivates us by its sheer beauty. Somehow, the vicissitudes of our lives pale beside the boldness, or delicateness, of nature's handiwork.

The park is a genuine wilderness, and much of it can only be reached on foot. Backcountry travel is made easier and safer by six hundred miles of trails. You could hike these trails for two solid months and always be seeing new country. And should you choose to head cross-country instead, you would learn first-hand why the Olympic Peninsula remained unconquered for so long.

The Olympic wilderness can be experienced on many other levels. Spur roads lead to many major attractions, like the Hoh and Quinault rain forests, Kalaloch and Rialto beaches, and the magnificent views of Hurricane Ridge. Scattered around the park are enclaves of resorts, campgrounds, and interpretive centers. Beauty, mystery, and adventure beckon everywhere. The wilderness calls with many voices, for Olympic National Park is a vast and varied treasure.

ED COOPER

A glacier is essentially compacted snow. Glaciers start when the snow fall exceeds the snow melt. As centuries pass, nature sculpts the ice into varied shapes and forms.

From the Hoh Rain Forest Visitor Center *one can venture into a magnificent temperate rain forest where you will experience a unique three-dimensional world of green.*

Olympic National Park presents three dramatic views of nature at work. From the glaciers to the rain forest and down to the sea. Even at the coastline the forces can be brutal. Seastacks abound, tidepools contain varied life often in selective layers. Take the time to see the small creatures too!

When these heavy oceanic plates collide with the continental plates, something has to give.

The Master Architect

TOM & PAT LEESON

When we gaze upon the towering rugged mountains of Olympic, they seem to have an aura of permanency about them. But the atomic-sized blast, which reshaped nearby Mount Saint Helens dramatically, destroyed this illusion.

Overwhelming evidence has recently been uncovered indicating the earth is not a stable mass, but an extremely dynamic one undergoing relentless change. Most geologists now believe that the earth's surface consists of gigantic plates floating on a layer of dense molten rock so hot it moves in slow currents across the mantle. To visualize this, imagine a large pot of thick soup over a small burner. Convection currents are set up as the warm soup in the center rises to the top, moving the cooler surface material to the side, where it descends. If you dropped a cracker into the center, it would be transported to the side. The earth's plates move like the cracker, but in a slower fashion.

Due to such convection currents, plates of the ocean floor are sometimes pulled apart near undersea ridges and moved toward the continents. As the plates move away from the ridges, lava emerges to caulk the cracks in the ridges or erupts into flows on the bottom; either way, basalt lava forms the oceanic plates.

When these heavy oceanic plates collide with the continental plates, something has to give. Usually, the heavy oceanic plates dip beneath the lighter continental plates in zones of convergence and subduction. In such zones, faulting occurs and further inland molten rock often rises to the surface forming volcanoes. Several volcanoes are still active in the Cascade Range, indicating that this process continues even today in the Pacific Northwest.

About fifty-five million years ago, what is now the Olympic Peninsula lay beneath the sea. Sediments washed out from the land accumulated on top of the sea floor; these were compressed by their own weight into shale and sandstone. Also, vents and fissures on the sea floor spewed out basalt lava, in some cases forming underwater mountains called seamounts. Some grew into islands. Several of these huge basalt domes formed on the sea floor off the coast.

Mountains and ridges affect distribution of rain and fog in the Olympics.

Some thirty million years ago, the oceanic plate was inching toward the continent from the Juan de Fuca Ridge. Most of the oceanic plate descended beneath the continental plate in a subduction zone located between the present Olympic Mountains and the Cascades. Because the undersea ridge was relatively close to the coast at the time, the oceanic plate had less time to cool than if it had had a longer distance to travel before meeting the continent. Consequently, it remained more buoyant and did not sink as easily under the continental plate as the material that preceded it.

As convection currents continued pushing the oceanic plate under the continent, sedimentary material seaward of the volcanic pile was jammed beneath it, causing the pile to rise while the oceanic plate warped downward. Tremendous forces folded, sliced, and contorted sedimentary rocks.

About twelve million years ago, the convection currents apparently stopped or slowed near the Olympics. Some geologists think the subduction zone shifted seaward over a hundred miles. Today, a low sloping subduction zone can be inferred from earthquake patterns under the Olympics.

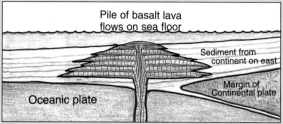

Pile of basalt lava flows on sea floor

Sediment from continent on east

Oceanic plate

Margin of Continental plate

A. 30-55 million years ago.

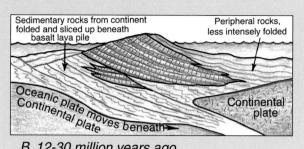

Sedimentary rocks from continent folded and sliced up beneath basalt lava pile

Peripheral rocks, less intensely folded

Oceanic plate moves beneath Continental plate

Continental plate

B. 12-30 million years ago.

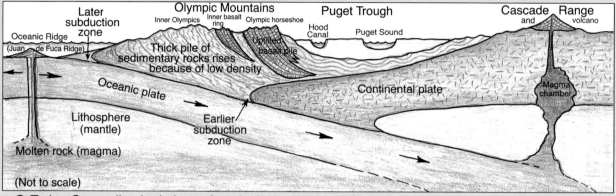

Later subduction zone

Olympic Mountains

Inner Olympics Inner basalt ring Olympic horseshoe

Puget Trough

Cascade Range and volcano

Oceanic Ridge (Juan de Fuca Ridge)

Hood Canal Puget Sound

Thick pile of sedimentary rocks rises because of low density

Uplifted basalt pile

Oceanic plate

Continental plate

Magma chamber

Lithosphere (mantle)

Earlier subduction zone

Molten rock (magma)

(Not to scale)

C. Today. Generalized relations of geologic structures of Olympic Mountains, Puget Trough, and Cascade Range and volcano.

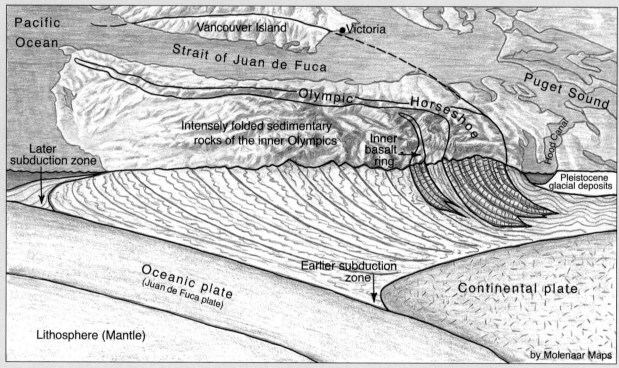

Pacific Ocean

Vancouver Island

Victoria

Strait of Juan de Fuca

Olympic

Horseshoe

Puget Sound

Intensely folded sedimentary rocks of the inner Olympics

Inner basalt ring

Hood Canal

Later subduction zone

Pleistocene glacial deposits

Oceanic plate (Juan de Fuca plate)

Earlier subduction zone

Continental plate

Lithosphere (Mantle)

by Molenaar Maps

D. West-to-east geologic section across the Olympic Penninsula, showing principal subduction zones related to the formation of the Olympic Mountains and the generalized topographic expressions of the underlying geologic structures.

Present-day visitors to the Olympics are rewarded by seeing striking patterns in the folded sedimentary rocks. And on Hurricane Ridge Road, lava has hardened into the pillow-shaped masses characteristic of having been formed beneath the sea. The park is one of the few places where such forms can be studied on land.

The formation of the Olympic Peninsula is an intricate and complex puzzle. Geologists are constantly reviewing and debating new evidence in an effort to better understand the origins of this fascinating place.

Inviting vistas beckon from the interior. *The rugged ridges and beautiful valleys are a result of geologic processes. Streams and glaciers have carved many of Nature's masterpieces.*

ED COOPER

The **formation** of the **Olympic** Peninsula is an **intricate** and complex **puzzle**.

The Bailey Range serves as one of the major barriers to moisture flowing in from the Pacific, creating a rain shadow to the northeast.

Sculpturing By Water and Ice

As the dome rose, it began to capture moisture from the Pacific. Streams formed, radiating in all directions from the center, which was near the beginning of the present Elwha River. This river, and the glaciers that later filled the valley, eventually carved the heart of the dome. All the other rivers likewise formed valleys.

Erosion sculptured the Olympics into remarkable patterns. Shales and slates were the least resistant and succumbed first, followed by sandstone. Basalt endured the longest. Areas with steep slopes and faults eroded faster than more level stretches. Erosion dramatically sped up during the last two million years, when North America was in the grips of the great Ice Age. During this period, almost a third of the continent was covered by massive bodies of glacial ice.

One form of ice consisted of vast sheets which spread across Canada and extended into the northern United States. Tongues of this ice penetrated northwestern Washington at least six times. As the ice jammed up against the Olympic Mountains, one part branched toward the sea, carving out what is now the Strait of Juan de Fuca. The other flowed down the east side, forming Puget Sound. Thus the Olympics were virtually isolated from the rest of North America by ice.

Ice also took the form of alpine glaciers similar to those seen today. These filled and broadened the great valleys formed earlier by streams, sculpturing the Olympics into the dramatic scenery that exists today.

Some thirteen thousand years ago, the climate grew warmer. Most alpine glaciers melted before the last retreat of the continental ice sheet, which continued to dam several valley drainages, forming huge lakes. These ice sheets had carried rocks of granite, gneiss, and schist, foreign to the Olympics, in from Canada. As icebergs broke off and floated up the lakes, they deposited these foreign rocks high in the Olympic Mountains where they still can be found.

Most of today's glaciers probably formed about twenty-five hundred years ago, although large glaciers, like the Blue and Hoh, may have survived from the Ice Age.

High mountains and steep slopes create avalanche conditions. Snow avalanches can create scenes like this. Trees like the Sitka alder and Alaska cedar are able to withstand snow creep and avalanching because of their limber branches.

ED COOPER

A dark black line indicates that two glaciers have joined, forming a larger one. Rock debris falling on the sides of glaciers form what is known as lateral moraines. When the glaciers combine, the two lateral moraines become a single medial moraine.

ED COOPER

Olympic National Park is full of
spectacular scenery. The lake and
the cirque in the upper left were
carved by glaciers.

A GIFT OF THE SEA

The Olympic Mountains are not exceptionally
high. Mount Olympus, the highest, is just less than
eight thousand feet. But their impressive breadth,
as well as their closeness to the sea, makes them
special. In fact, Olympic has been called a gift of the
sea, for the huge dome that was the forerunner of
the Olympics rose out of the sea. And the almost
four thousand square miles of serrated peaks and
valleys carved from it are nearly surrounded by
seawater. The Pacific reigns supreme on the west,
while the Strait of Juan de Fuca, Puget Sound, and
Hood Canal occupy old glacial troughs.

The high country is a good place to
see the tilted rock formations created
when the Olympic Mountains floated
to their present heights.

The effect of the sea is subtle in the mountainous regions of the park. As moisture-laden clouds generated at sea move inward, they strike the Olympics. As they flow over the mountains, moisture condenses from them. The western slopes and valleys are deluged with a staggering one hundred forty inches of rain each year – or nearly twelve feet! Fog also creeps up the valleys frequently, keeping the climate moist. The summit of Mount Olympus receives some two hundred inches of precipitation, which falls mostly as snow. Precipitation is measured by water content, so light, air-filled snowflakes can build a layer as much as a hundred feet deep. Because more snow falls in the higher elevations than melts in most years, the snow accumulates, compacts under its own weight, and forms glaciers.

The clouds travel east, continuing to lose moisture until at Sequim (pronounced "squim"), protected by the rain shadow of the Olympic Mountains, only fifteen or twenty inches fall. Only forty miles separates the wettest spot in North America from Sequim, where farmers must irrigate the land to support their crops.

The clouds that sneak around the southern end of the Olympics retain more moisture, so Staircase, to the southeast, boasts some one hundred inches of rainfall, supporting a forest similar to the true rain forests of the western slope.

ED COOPER

The avalanche lily is one of the first flowers to decorate
the high meadows and slopes after the snow melts.

ED COOPER

Glaciers are nature's bulldozers. They carve out natural amphitheaters called cirques, and widen streambeds into U-shaped valleys. The white-flowered Merten's cassiope and the red mountain heath are two high country heathers.

The land has been terraced down to the rivers
by past glacial advances and retreats,
and by streams which deposited gravel
and then cut new channels.

The Great Forests of Olympic

Olympic National Park encompasses the greatest remaining true wilderness forest in the contiguous United States. Record-size specimens of several species of trees testify to the ideal conditions for growth. The plants of this region, and to a lesser degree the animals, tend to group themselves into diverse communities, their location often dictated by climate. Toward either pole and toward higher elevations, temperatures drop. But at Olympic, the ocean has a moderating effect on temperatures, while the mountains dramatically influence weather patterns. Even fire affects the distribution of plants.

THE TEMPERATE RAIN FOREST

Take a mild coastal climate, add a good dose of rain and fog, and you have the ingredients for a temperate rain forest. (Some biologists call this forest the Sitka spruce zone instead, because this tree is so prevalent, but western hemlock, western red cedar, and bigleaf maple are also important constituents here.)

Sitka spruce grows in a narrow band along the coast and up the river valleys from Alaska to southern Oregon, where it blends into the redwood forests. On the Olympic Peninsula, this band of spruce is wider because of the broad coastal plain.

Bigleaf maple branches decorated with clubmoss draperies and bright green licorice ferns are special favorites with visitors.

Western red cedar grows in limited numbers in the rain forest, although it may form pure stands, called cedar swamps, in moist soil. The attractive bark of these massive trees adds color and character to the forest.

DAVID MUENCH

ED COOPER

-14-

Sitka spruce, the dominant tree in the temperate rain forest, grows from Alaska to northern California.

On offshore sea stacks and along the coast, wind, sand, and spray batter Sitka spruce into gnarled shapes. Huge burls sometimes develop in the trunks of these trees, possibly caused by fungi, insects or bacteria. It affects the tree's structure, but does not kill it..

The shore pine, a lowland variety of lodgepole pine, also grows near the coast, as well as in marshy or gravelly sites where other trees cannot dominate the soil. (The upland variety of lodgepole pine grows in poor soil conditions at higher elevations; neither variety normally grows at middle elevations.)

Inland, protected from the salt spray, western hemlock and red cedar are major trees of the rain forest, although Douglas-fir may thrive where fire or massive windstorms have opened clearings.

Western hemlock is the truest rival of Sitka spruce. It produces more seeds than Sitka spruce and can reproduce more efficiently in dense shade, so theoretically it should dominate this zone.

But forests are more than a collection of trees. Roosevelt elk, an integral part of Olympic National Park, feed on young hemlock trees—not on young Sitka spruce. Also, Sitka spruce seem to be more tolerant of the occasional flooding near the rivers. Thus grazing elk and flooding, as well as climatic conditions, seem to favor the Sitka spruce. On the western-facing slopes, western hemlock does not dominate until above one thousand feet, although it is the dominant tree down to sea level on the east side.

WILLIS PETERSON

Vine maple leaves form beautiful patterns. Vine maples, important temperate rain forest trees, often spread out their branches like the tentacles of an octopus. Elk and deer browse on such shrubs, thus maintaining clearings in the forest.

ROSS HAMILTON/APERTURE

Although this scene of Douglas-fir western hemlock, and vanilla leaf was taken in the rain forest, it is more typical of lowland forest.

Seedlings of the giant trees of the forest have trouble getting started on the densely carpeted forest floor, so they established themselves on slightly decayed nurse logs. After the nurse log rots, the trees that grew on the nurse log remain standing in a row called a colonnade.

Red cedar sometimes forms pure stands in moist soils. Cedar swamps once were fairly common in poorly drained stretches near the ocean, but most of these great stands were logged years ago. Unfortunately, this beautiful tree is rapidly becoming a thing of the past outside the park. On less moist soils, red cedar must compete with other trees for space and is not nearly as prevalent, but its massive trunks, stringy fibrous bark, and aromatic boughs have so much character that they add seasoning to the forest.

DAVID MUENCH

Hemlock boughs, especially from young trees, are one of the elk's preferred foods.

The Rain Forest

The temperate rain forest is as much an artistic concept as it is a biological one. In the text, the term is applied to the entire Sitka spruce forest for simplicity, but usually it is used for a rain forest only when it grows in western-facing valleys.

The temperate rain forest is characterized by heavy rainfall, summer fogs, mosses in profusion, nurse logs, colonnades, trees standing on stilts, and bigleaf maples with spikemoss draperies and licorice ferns gowing on them.

Elk, deer, and other animals are an integral part of Olympic's rain forest and their sights and sounds add much to the texture of this very special place.

Your imagination is stimulated in the temperate rain forest. A moss-draped lower limb can remind you of an ancient creature.

RAY ATKESON

In the southwestern-facing Hoh, Queets, and Quinault valleys, the temperate rain forest is especially noteworthy. These steep, flat-bottomed valleys trap fog, keeping the weather mild and providing moisture during the fairly dry summers. Here, colonnades of Sitka spruce and western hemlock grow, some trees stand on stilts, huge maples are covered with draperies of spikemoss, and even the air seems to have turned green. Mosses are everywhere, contributing to the distinctive personality of this rain forest.

The land has been terraced down to the rivers by past glacial advances and retreats, and by streams which deposited gravel and then cut new channels.

Red alder is the most common tree on river terraces. They are important pioneer plants because of their ability to increase the nitrogen content of the soil.

On lower terraces, where periodic flooding occurs, communities of Sitka spruce, bigleaf maple, and black cottonwood may develop.

Farther from the rivers, and on the higher terraces, the moss-dominated rain forest of Sitka spruce and western hemlock grows. Bigleaf maple grows mostly in disturbed sites, but it is so picturesque that it typifies the rain forest to many people. Vine maple also grows here, spreading its branches out like the tentacles of an octopus.

Ironically, the tiny seeds of the giant forest monarchs do not seem to be able to gain a foothold

Spikemoss, licorice
fern and other epiphytes
(air plants) do not harm trees; some trees
even obtain nutrients from them.

ED COOPER

High densities of plants and intense
competition for space are common in the rain
forest. Licorice fern, maidenhair fern, trillium,
oxalis, huckleberry, sword fern, vine maple, and
trailing blackberry are some of the plants growing here.

WILLIS PETERSON

A quiet peace permeates
the temperate rain forest.
Small streams are
important nurseries
for small fish.

RAY ATKESON

on the ground. Perhaps other plants crowd them out, the environment is too acidic, or disease is responsible; no one is certain.

The huge trees are vulnerable in another respect: because of abundant moisture in the soil, the trees do not need deep roots. Thus they can be toppled by strong winds. Once the fallen trees begin to decay, they become ideal sites for seed germination. Small trees soon establish themselves on a log, but competition eventually reduces their numbers. Their success is dependent upon their ability to reach the soil, so their roots gradually creep down and around the nurse log until they reach the ground. The first plants that are able to tap nutrients in the soil gain a tremendous advantage over their competitors, and their chances of success are greatly increased. Survivors grow in a row like soldiers standing at attention. These colonnades are a hallmark of the temperate rain forest.

Sometimes the seedlings get a start in a stump or snag several feet tall, so their roots have much farther to grow to reach the ground. When the stumps decay and crumble, the living trees appear to be standing on stilts. Such trees are another hallmark of the temperate rain forest.

Glades of bigleaf maple grow in rocky soil within the older forest. *Epiphytes*—spikemosses, liverworts, lichens, and licorice fern—grow on these trees. These epiphytes may obtain some nutrition from decaying bark, but most nourishment comes from sunlight, airborne particles, and moisture.

The upshot is a fantasy land of eighty-foot trees adorned with draperies of moss. Cathedrals of green are formed, the moss-laden limbs stretching up to forty feet long and weighing up to a ton. Except for the tremendous weight of the epiphytes, which can cause limbs to break and trees to fall, the epiphytes are not harmful. They can be beneficial, in fact, for some bigleaf maples send roots into the thick mats of epiphytes to feed on airborne nutrients captured there. These glades of bigleaf maple are the third hallmark of these forests.

THE LOWLAND FOREST

Above the temperate rain forest of the coast, and growing as the lowest forest of the rest of the peninsula, is the lowland forest, identified by the following combination of trees. First, grand fir replaces Sitka spruce below a thousand feet, although an occasional spruce may grow in this zone. Western hemlock becomes the most dominant tree in the mature lowland forest, while red cedar, another prevalent species, can be used as an indicator for this zone.

Somewhere between two and three thousand feet in elevation red cedar ceases to be a common

JEFF GNASS

***D**ouglas-firs are much more common in lowland and montane forests that might be expected. Periodic fires and drier soil conditions, especially on southern slopes of the northeastern part of the park, contribute to this distribution.*

element of the forest, although wind patterns along some river valleys may allow it to grow several hundred feet higher upslope. The decrease in occurrence of red cedar can be used to mark the upper limit of the lowland forest.

Red alder grows on river terraces, and young grand fir grows underneath it, instead of Sitka spruce. Good examples of this can be seen at Staircase and Dosewallips campgrounds. Extensive Douglas-fir stands flourish where fires have burned away large areas, because the corky bark of Douglas-fir, up to a foot thick, enables it to withstand fire better than other trees. Sprinkled throughout drier stands of Douglas-fir is the Pacific madrone. Its bright orange bark adds a beautiful contrast to the scene.

Small trees soon establish themselves but competition eventually reduces their numbers.

ROSS HAMILTON/APERTURE

At first glance, this looks like a subalpine forest, but the meadow in the foreground is likely the result of avalanches. The continuous wooded area in the distance is probably mostly montane forest. From a distance it is not easy to distinguish life zones because the lowland, montane, and lower part of the subalpine forests have a continuous cover of trees.

Mountain hemlocks frame a subalpine lake formed by glacial plucking, a process in which large boulders are pulled out of the ground by ice.

Mountain hemlock cones produce plenty of seeds. The seedlings do well in glacially carved bowls with abundant winter snows.

Woodland pinedrops, a saprophyte which lives on decaying matter, lacks chlorophyll. It cannot manufacture its own food as green plants do, so it feeds on decaying matter on the forest floor.

THE MONTANE FOREST

The montane zone begins around two or three thousand feet in the central Olympics. This zone is wetter and colder than the lowland forest. More precipitation falls as snow, which may accumulate to eight feet deep.

Many botanists call this zone and the lower part of the next the silver fir zone. In the western part of the park, silver fir dominates the higher elevations, while western hemlock prevails at lower elevations. But in much of the east, Douglas-fir becomes prevalent. And in the northeast, in areas like Hurricane Ridge and Deer Park, silver fir is absent except in cold pockets near Heart O' the Hills Campground and other isolated spots.

The primary cause of this uneven distribution on silver fir is the rain-shadow effect of the mountains. Silver fir requires a cool, wet climate, so it does not thrive in the dry northeastern Olympics. But at Dosewallips River, to the southeast, conditions are tolerable and silver fir reappears. Silver fir, and western hemlock, have thin bark and are susceptible to fire, which is a factor favoring Douglas-fir in many stands east of the Bailey Range.

ED COOPER

Splotches of lichens form patterns on red alder bark. Red alder is a pioneer tree that grows in quickly after fires, and rapidly invades gravel bars along the sides of streams. In the rain forest, Sitka spruce may be seen growing under mature stands of alder along the sides of streams. In the lowland forest, grand fir may grow under alder.

The lower limits of silver fir seem to be controlled by temperature. At lower elevations where temperatures are warmer and most precipitation falls as rain, lowland forest trees do better. On the other hand, the coolness of the montane zone gives silver fir an edge over these species. Coldness slows decay and causes organic matter to accumulate, through which the roots of the silver fir seedlings can penetrate and tap soil more effectively. Moreover, silver fir seeds can germinate and their seedlings grow in near freezing soil conditions.

At its upper limits silver fir gives way to trees such as subalpine fir and mountain hemlock which are even better adapted to short growing seasons and heavy winter snows.

Overleaf: The high country is covered with snow most of the year. Photo by Pat O'Hara.

The trees in this fierce and cold world are fascinating.

ROSS HAMILTON/APERTURE

The cathedral-spire shape of the subalpine fir helps shed winter snows. The tree is limbed to the ground, which increases the likelihood of burning if a lightning fire starts. Fire helps create subalpine meadows, and heavy snows help maintain them.

THE SUBALPINE FOREST

Snowmelt is a key factor influencing the transition from montane to subalpine forest. Snow packs up to thirty feet deep and lower temperatures mean that snow lasts into July in the subalpine zone, whereas the montane zone is free of snow by early June. The rain shadow effect continues to be important even at these high altitudes.

West of Mount Olympus, where the influence of the sea is felt and slopes are gentle, subalpine forests are rare. Most ridges are not high enough to support such a forest. The headwaters of the Bogachiel River form the western limit of this zone.

Although lowland forests extend farther up valleys than slopes, the opposite is true of subalpine forests. Instead, cold air flows down the valleys, lowering temperatures and permitting subalpine trees to grow in the montane zone. Snow avalanches enhance this by transporting seeds. And the ocean moderates environmental differences normally associated with elevation changes. Because of these factors, separations between zones are less distinct west of the Bailey Range.

In the central Olympics, thirty-six hundred feet is the normal limit for western hemlock, red cedar, western white pine, and Douglas-fir. This also marks the approximate lower limit of subalpine fir, mountain hemlock, and yellow or Alaska

The upper portion of subalpine forest east of the Bailey Range consists of clumps of trees intermingled with meadows. This growth pattern reflects an intense struggle for survival. Either too much or too little snow can kill the tree seedlings. Subalpine trees often develop skirts under a protective layer of snow. These lower branches may take root.

cedar. This striking boundary is used by some botanists to separate the montane and subalpine forests in this region.

In the northeastern part of the park, however, the subalpine zone starts at forty-five hundred feet or higher. Because this area is drier, Douglas-fir grows to the timberline alongside subalpine trees. Lodgepole pine is common on Blue Mountain.

The lower portion of the subalpine zone is covered by forests. Higher up, the wind is very strong, the soil is frozen, and the weight of the snow crushes frail trees. The ability of the trees to survive here is tested to the limit. Meadows can dominate large sections, resulting in clumps of trees delightfully intermingled with picturesque meadows.

The trees in this fierce world are fascinating. A three-inch-thick specimen may be a hundred years old. Bitter winds may batter trees to the typical height of the snow packs, forming twisted dwarf shrubs known as Krummholzes. One Alaska cedar Krummholz in the park, which may be a thousand years old, is only three feet high, yet sprawls out some fifty feet in diameter. Another Alaska cedar tree is thought to be twice as old, maybe older.

Subalpine fir, mountain hemlock, and Alaska cedar can reproduce by layering: lower branches, pressed to the ground by snow, take root and form new trees. When the parent tree dies, the offspring form circular clusters known as timber atolls.

Subalpine fir, the most widespread true fir in western North America, is particularly suited for growth in deep snow. It is limbed to the ground with short length branches. It sheds snow like the A-frame roof of a chalet. The lower branches, often

*S*ilky phacelia likes dry sunny, open slopes.

*P*iper bellflower grows
only in Olympic.

protected by snow from destructive blizzards, tend to grow into plush skirts around the base of the tree. These branches may even take root, although the broad base makes subalpine fir quite vulnerable to fire.

Mountain hemlock and Alaska cedar, as well as subalpine fir, are also susceptible to fire because of their thin bark. Although forest fires are rare here, the destruction of trees is almost inevitable when a blaze does occur. Afterwards, harsh climatic conditions retard the new growth. In a sense, fires create meadows and snow conditions perpetuate them.

Subalpine trees walk a teeter-totter of environmental stress. Heavy snow damages small seedlings, but on windswept ridges, trees will die because they cannot drink moisture from the frozen soil. These trees are largely dependent on snowmelt for water. If the wind sweeps away the snow, warm temperatures and blistering breezes will cause trees to die of thirst. If a snow pack is too deep, however, it can take too long to melt, and the growing season may be too short for the trees to complete their reproductive cycle. On the other hand, lack of a protective snow blanket may subject trees to the blasting effects of windblown snow. Trees that manage to live in this harsh region emphasize the struggle for survival that all creatures in the wild face.

ALPINE MEADOWS

Above the subalpine zone, conditions are too fierce for trees to survive. The snow lasts into August, so the growing season is too short for seedlings to get a start. Some meadows thrive about the timberline, although most of the alpine zone is steep and rugged. Bare rocks, permanent snowfields, and glaciers characterize the highest domes and basins.

Plants hug the ground. All are perennials because the growing seasons are too short for them to start from a seed, grow, flower, and ripen their seeds in one season. Many have small tough leaves covered with hair or wax to help prevent moisture loss during high winds or warm summer days. Summer visitors are rewarded with breathtaking scenery topped off with vivid displays of wildflowers.

FOREST FIRES

Man-caused fires start every year in the park, but very few acres have burned due to effective firefighting efforts. Indians may have used fires to maintain a few prairies within the park, but the area affected was small.

Lightning is the primary cause of fires that significantly influence the vegetation, once again, the rain shadow effect of the Bailey Range is felt; almost ninety percent of the lightning fires occur in the eastern portion of the park. Over eighty percent of these start above three thousand feet, mainly because lightning is most apt to strike there.

Thunderstorms are a normal component of Olympic weather, but most of them do not produce lightning. Also, low temperatures, moist vegetation, and rain help to prevent fires from starting. About every three years, some fires do start, but

The struggle for survival continues throughout the park, but sometimes it is more easily recognized in the high country. Here, a subalpine fir grows on a rocky ledge beneath a snag. The snag is probably the victim of environmental stress, although lightning may have killed it. Spotted saxifrage, growing in the foreground, lives on rocky ledges near and above the timberline.

GLENN VAN NIMWEGEN

most occur every ten years or so between July and early September. Major fires have periodically occurred every one to three hundred years.

Even when fires do strike, the forest recovers swiftly, and young stands of sub-dominant trees emerge. Thus, some western white pines in the montane zone actually owe their existence to fire, while Douglas-firs persist in areas normally dominated by other trees. Natural fires are essential to Olympic's forests. Therefore, in the future, the Park will allow more natural fires to run their course.

SUGGESTED READING

ARNO, STEVEN F. AND RAMONA P. HAMMERLY. *Northwest Trees*. Seattle: Seattle Mountaineers, 1977.

KIRK, RUTH. T*he Olympic Rain Forest: An Ecological Web*. Seattle: University of Washington Press, 1992.

MATHEWS, DANIEL. *Cascade-Olympic Natural History*. Portland, Oregon: Raven Editions, 1988.

STEWART, CHARLES. *Wildflowers of the Olympics*. San Francisco: Nature Education Enterprises, 1972.

The brutality and violence of their world
fascinates and perturbs us.
One moment can be full of tenderness and peace,
the next, brimming with terror.

The Wildlife of Olympic

Some animals move with regal grace, others as if life were one great comedy. A few appear awkward and clumsy. All are alert and wary. Animals are an integral part of the wilderness and a cherished part of our heritage.

The brutality and violence of their world fascinates and perturbs us. One moment can be full of tenderness and peace, the next, brimming with terror. We are intrigued by the animals. They amuse us, perplex us, repulse us, and stir a feeling of kinship within us.

The call of the wild has many voices: it can be as quiet as a gentle breeze, as musical as the song of a bird, or as compelling as a primal summons. Hearing the bugling of a Roosevelt elk is an experience most travelers treasure because it reverberates with the essence of the wilderness.

ROSS HAMILTON

Olympic marmots are a product of Ice Age isolation and are found only in the Olympics. Males normally mate with two females who bear young in alternating years.

Competition is keen in these Olympic games. Over 800 pounds of bull on either side fights for a cow, or harem of cows, in the autumn rut. One bull will prevail, his sharply pointed antlers thrusting the most power. Exhausted, the victor will collect his spoils. The defeated bull will either remain nearby as an outrider, compete for another herd, or just surrender to his losses and depart.

THE ROOSEVELT ELK

A majestic bull elk, sporting a twenty-pound rack of antlers, makes a regal sight at the onset of the breeding cycle, or rut, which begins in September. Bulls, which weigh up to a thousand pounds or more, begin to wander restlessly, violently thrashing trees and shrubs to flex their muscles and mark out their territories.

Each bull strives to round up and breed his own herd of cows. Once a bull succeeds, he guards them closely, traveling behind the herd, always alert for strays which he quickly drives back into the fold. Throughout the rut, the bull periodically emits high-pitched, piercing screams known as bugling.

Two- or three-year-old bulls, known as outriders, may attempt to join the herd, either because of their budding desires or because they still wish to be with their mothers. They are rudely driven off by the master, however. But when one big bull is challenged by another, the excitement really begins. A fierce winner-take-all battle ensues and the clash of antlers sounds throughout the woods. One or both of the combatants occasionally dies from the battle.

The victorious bull may stay with his harem until early winter, but his interest usually turns to food and rest by October. Eventually the gaunt bull drifts away from the herd, seeking a safe shelter of thickets to recuperate in. Other bulls may congregate with him. The bulls sometimes remain together as a bachelor herd until they repeat the rutting cycle next fall.

Cows and offspring, including bulls four or even five years old, normally travel in herds of fifteen to over a hundred. Each herd is usually led by older cows. The herds are often composed of the offspring of related females.

Frequent calls and squeals are normal as the herds move, especially when cows and calves enter dense thickets. They can easily pass through brush that is seemingly impenetrable to us. They play a key role in mowing down shrubbery and maintaining clearings in the forests, as mentioned in the preceding chapter.

Columbia black-tailed deer are a subspecies of the mule deer. They readily become accustomed to visitors and look harmless, but an unexpected blow from their sharp hooves can cause serious injury, especially to children.

In spring, some elk feed on the tender young grass of the lowlands, while other migrate into higher meadows. After the grass ages and toughens in summer, the elk begin to browse on trees and shrubs for food.

Some elk remain in the valleys all year but often use the more densely forested south-facing slopes during winter, presumably because the thick canopy of trees reduces the amount of snow that reaches the ground. The heavy forest also provides a buffer against chilling winds. Moreover, the southern exposure has more sunlight and snow melt.

Malnutrition and other hardships associated with winter are the leading causes of death to elk. About ten times as many elk die from the grueling winter as are killed by predators.

The main predator of elk is the cougar, although its diet consists mostly of rabbits and deer, which are easier to catch and kill. A cougar usually will not attack a healthy adult, although it will pull down a weak one or a calf. Coyotes and bears occasionally prey upon calves also, although bears are more likely to eat carrion. The elk's first defense is to run, but it can become a formidable opponent if cornered. Its forefeet are lethal, and it can use its antlers effectively.

UNUSUAL MAMMALS OF OLYMPIC

When a whistle pierces the air, you know you are in marmot territory. These wonderful relatives of the eastern woodchuck are Olympic's largest squirrel. They live in the high meadows or talus slopes of Olympic and are found nowhere else in the world. The marmots feed upon wildflowers, which frequently adorn the meadows and grasses and sedges. They also occasionally eat meat.

The chatter and scolding of Douglas squirrels are among the great sounds of the wilderness. Middens of conifer cone scales in the woods indicate the presence of these fascinating creatures.

TOM & PAT LEESON

STOUFFER PRODUCTIONS/ANIMALS ANIMALS

The Olympic short-tailed weasel is found nowhere else in the world.

DIANE ENSIGN-CAUGHEY

The Olympic chipmunk lives only in the Olympics.

Marmot life centers around the colony. Ten or twelve individuals usually live in each: an adult male, two adult females, a few yearlings belonging to one of the females, and some youngsters belonging to the other. This unusual arrangement works well because the females normally breed every other year.

Olympic marmots are gregarious animals who greet each other with kisses, play, and fight. Their whistles alert or warn others when danger threatens so they can seek refuge in one of many burrows. A burrow may go down fifteen feet and contain separate chambers for food, storage, and sleeping.

Marmots escape the ravages of winter by hibernating. Before retiring, however, they sometimes double their body weight with fat. Once they go into deep sleep, their heart rate may slow to two beats a minute. Although their coats are black when they hibernate, they can be considerably lighter when they emerge in spring, perhaps because of the bleaching action of ammonia from urine excreted in the den.

The Olympic short-tailed weasel, also found here, does not turn white during winter, as short-tailed weasels elsewhere do, although its coat does get a little lighter. Apparently after the Ice Age, the Olympics were populated with weasels from the lowlands, where winter snow was not a controlling factor in survival camouflage. That Olympic forests are dense and dark may also be a factor. The snow-shoe or varying hare also changes color throughout most of its range but does not in the Olympics.

The Olympic chipmunk inhabits the subalpine zone, where the forest opens into parklands. It is larger and duller colored than its close relations elsewhere. The Townsend chipmunks, not an endemic, live in the lower denser forest and are also dark.

The Olympic Mazama pocket gopher lives in the soil of the subalpine zone of the Olympics. It is active all winter, foraging in tunnels under the snow, feeding on the roots of grass and other plants. As the snow melts, the pocket gopher burrows underground, pushing earth up into the snow, forming long castings on the surface which fascinate summer visitors.

Easily overlooked, the red-legged frog of the Olympics proves to be quite colorful.

The Olympic snow mole is another creature whose relatives are common in lower elevations. But the snow mole lives high on Hurricane Ridge, where it forages in snow tunnels during the winter, also leaving snow castings.

One time, some excited citizens, who had lived in the woods all their lives, saw Bigfoot tracks on a logging road. Investigation revealed a long series of giant humanlike tracks. Fortunately, the culprit became obvious at the end of the tracks. A black bear had placed its hind foot closely in front of its forefoot when walking. The claw marks didn't show until near the end of the trail.

The Columbian black-tailed deer is the smallest subspecies of mule deer. Its gentle demeanor attracts visitors although it can slash viciously with its front hooves if threatened. It is not a true herd animal, but several may graze together. In the fall, bucks, like bull elks, grow antlers and gather harems.

Anyone who has often camped in the backcountry knows it is a bad mistake to overlook small rodents like shrews, voles, deer mice, and woodrats. These creatures have a proven ability to walk the high wire, eating through expensive backpacks wired hopefully from trees to keep animals from reaching the food in them. Many other interesting animals, like flying squirrels, black bear, and bobcats, roam the park.

Eleven mammals found in nearby areas in Washington and British Columbia are not native to the park because of its history of isolation. These include the grizzly, wolverine, mountain sheep, lynx, pika, golden-mantled ground squirrel, water vole, bog lemming, red fox, porcupine, and mountain goat.

The red fox and porcupine have invaded the southern part of the peninsula recently, however, and are gradually moving toward the park, apparently because of a natural population spread. Mountain goats were introduced in the late 1920s and have spread throughout much of the park. They represent a serious management problem because they harm the ecology.

THE FREE SPIRITS

Birds are free spirits who soar, hop, and dart, adding music to the wilderness with their calls and songs.

The gray-crowned rosy finch inhabits alpine cirques—natural amphitheaters—and meadows during summer. The horned lark may be seen walking on snow patches or alpine meadows. The

River otters are common on the peninsula and are often mistaken for sea otters.

Blue herons are large birds with six-foot wingspans. They are easily recognized in flight by their folded necks and trailing legs. They often stand knee-deep in water.

dark-eyed junco frequents forest edges, while the rufous hummingbird feeds on nectar along the sides of streams and in upland forest clearings. The red-tailed hawk soars overhead. The raven roams everywhere, but it is especially noticeable along the coast and on Hurricane Ridge.

The blue grouse is also often seen on Hurricane Ridge. The booming, hooting, ventriloquial sounds made by the male's inflated neck sacs during courtship can be heard in the lower woodlands as well. The ruffed grouse is common in deciduous woodlands and thickets, where it uses its wings to create a distinctive drumming sound to attract its mate.

The crow-sized pileated woodpecker carves out large rectangular holes in trees and stumps. The varied thrush, which looks like a robin with a black V on its chest, adds a haunting whistle to the forest. The winter wren may be the most commonly heard bird of the lowlands, for it emits a rapid succession of high tinkling warbles and trills.

Anyone who has camped in the backcountry knows it is a bad mistake to overlook small rodents.

The water ouzel or dipper fascinates observers as it bobs up and down on boulders in a stream, then dives under water to feed. Harlequin and merganser ducks float on the surface. The belted kingfisher zips along at tree height, issuing a loud high rattling call. The great blue heron walks knee deep in the water or flies with its neck crooked in an S shape. And, on lofty branches of Sitka spruce, bald eagles, those grand symbols of our nation, eye their coastal domain for tasty morsels of seafood.

None of the seventeen or more amphibians and reptiles of Olympic National Park are poisonous. Most are quite unobtrusive because they blend in so well with their surroundings. Once they are discovered, however, they often prove to be surprisingly bright-colored.

Ten common freshwater fish are found throughout Olympic. Lake Crescent once contained two varieties of native trout: the Beardslee and crescenti, which were found nowhere else. Unfortunately, the stock was contaminated by plantings of hatchery fish before the park was created. Trying to maintain a pure native population is one of the most difficult park challenges.

*T*o attract a mate, male ruffed grouse use their wings, creating a sound called drumming.

SUGGESTED READING

LARRISON, EARL J. *Mammals of the Northwest:* Washington, Oregon, Idaho and British Columbia. Seattle: Seattle Audubon Society, 1976.

MURIE, OLAUS J. *A Field Guide to Animal Tracks.* (Peterson Field Guide Series) 2nd ed. Boston: Houghton Mifflin Co., 1975.

WILDLIFE MANAGEMENT INSTITUTE. *Elk of North America* Harrisburg, Pennsylvania: Stockpole Books, 1982.

*A*n abundance of black oystercatchers is a sign of healthy coastal conditions

Flowers of Olympic

Plants brighten the wilderness with splashes of color. Their many hues call to mind the old adage: "If eyes were made for seeing, then beauty is its own excuse for being." Only a few of Olympic's wildflowers are shown here, for hundreds of varieties are spread from seashore to mountain top. Because of the varied landscape, spring seems to occur several times each year. As wildflowers fade in one location, a new display bursts forth at a higher elevation or on a different slope. Trees, shrubs, wildflowers, grasses, lichens, and other plants contribute to these eye-pleasing mosaics. Some of these high country plants can be seen only in the Olympics.

TOM & PAT LEESON

Beargrass and lupine

Lupine

GLENN VAN NIMWEGEN

KEITH GUNNAR

Sand-dwelling wallflower

Goatsbeard

Magenta paintbrush

Calypso orchid

Monkey flower

Glacier lily

Spreading phlox

*S*tonecrop

*F*ruiting head of
western pasque flower

*C*olumbia tiger lily

*D*ogwood blossoms

*L*ichens

The intertidal zone is an ideal place
to study nature because the patterns of life
are compressed into such small spaces.
The display of color and form in this region is magnificent.

The Teeming Seashore

Steep cliffs, sandy beaches with logs and drift-wood strewn about, waves crashing into head-lands or washing gently up sloping shores, sea stacks and water-sculptured arches, a gray whale blowing or a ship passing, the sea blending into the sky—all this culminates in a feeling of exhilaration mingled with peace, freedom, and a sense of the awesome power of the sea.

The plants and animals living on this coast might seem to have an easy life, for the ocean bathes them in a soup teeming with an almost infi-nite supply of food. The sea moderates the climate so temperature extremes are generally avoided. Nevertheless, living at the seashore is a very haz-ardous undertaking.

The vulnerability of these seashore organisms becomes apparent the more you learn. It makes you pause once you realize just one bite of a tasty purple-hinged rock scallop may represent ten or fifteen years of growth. Or what if you stepped on a green sea anemone, an animal that may live for a hundred years!

Sea otters were once native along the Washington coast, but were extirpated for their pelts. A small population was reintroduced in 1969, and occasionally a sea otter is seen floating on its back among kelp beds.

Sunsets and rock formations called seastacks combine with ocean sounds to create moods that defy description.

Seastacks were once part of the shore, but have been isolated by the sea, which continuously gnaws away softer rocks. When the tide is out, depressions in the rock form tidepools where many animals find refuge. The small kelp in the foreground is rockweed, an indicator plant of the upper intertidal zone.

The age of certain plants living on the seashore can be established more precisely. The woody stems of seaweed such as split kelp and Pterygophora (pronounced "tare-rig-GOF-for-uh") have rings as trees do. Moreover the rings on the shells of butter clams, cockles, and black turbans reflect seasonal variations in food supply and temperature. Marine organisms must adapt to these variations in environmental conditions, or they will perish.

Although the sea is serene at times, storms can whip waves into a frenzy, moving boulders weighing up to thirty-eight tons. Drifting logs also slam into beaches, killing some creatures and ripping others from their footholds. Even small waves are loaded with energy, for they overturn stones and shift sand. The surf, because of its burden of sand, scours rocks clean of all but the hardiest forms. All living organisms lying within reach of the waves must have some way of withstanding this steady onslaught. Nature has developed ingenious ways of ensuring the success of each species. The manner in which individual organisms have adapted to their environment, as well as the way they reproduce, is a fascinating study.

Recently, however, attention has turned to the ways various inhabitants interrelate with one another. An important step in this study is to group communities of organisms into zones. Since a greater concentration and variety of sea life thrives on rocky shores, we shall focus on the zones of the rocky intertidal regions. These zones, like terrestrial ones, exist in bands dictated by their height above sea level. The elevations of these bands are

Harbor seals are the most common *marine mammal along Olympic's coast. They are often seen sprawled out on rocky outcrops, which are the remnants of old seastacks, or swimming offshore. They are playful and curious, sometimes following hikers as they walk along the beach. Their diet includes fish, octopus, and crab.*

differentiated by only a few feet or even inches; their widths are determined to some extent by how steeply the shore slopes into the sea.

Plants and animals are not always rigidly restricted to a particular zone. Disturbance or the distribution of major species in a given area can radically alter the composition of communities within each zone.

On the Pacific coast, the seashore communities are exposed to two high tides and two low tides roughly every twenty-five hours. Thus the sea level routinely varies at least six feet a day at any given point and can vary as much as fifteen feet during the year.

The Spray Zone

The spray zone receives moisture from only the highest tides, the spray, and the rain. Temperatures fluctuate from literally freezing to downright hot. The salt content of the environment varies tremendously: rain dilutes it; evaporation concentrates it.

A low crusty growth of black lichens typically forms a horizontal band in the spray zone. Two species of barnacles cement themselves to the rocks: the little acorn barnacle and the common acorn barnacle, which is about three times larger. The common acorn barnacle can crowd out or crush its smaller neighbor; consequently, the little acorn barnacle is largely dependent on the action

The sea is serene at times. Storms can whip waves into a frenzy, moving boulders weighing many tons.

-43-

ROSS HAMILTON

ANNE WERTHEIM

Lacking a protective covering, hermit crabs crawl into empty snail shells. When the crabs grow too big, they trade in the old shells for new ones.

Nature imposes order upon the life on this boulder. Several patches of the green alga Prasiola grow in the upper left. A missed band of Pelvetiopsus and rainbow alga lies above whitish gooseneck barnacles. Below the gooseneck barnacles is sea moss, which looks dark brown. Next is a wide band of rockweed, which also grows below the tidepools in the foreground. Surfgrass grows in the tidepool to the right. A mixture of several other algae grows above the tidepools.

of waves, logs and other disturbances to remove the larger barnacle from the rocks, thus clearing areas for colonization.

Two tiny snails are common in the spray zone: the Sitka and the checkered periwinkle. The Sitka periwinkle favors sheltered cracks and moist areas, while the checkered periwinkle roves surfaces exposed to heavier spray. The finger limpet thrives in this region also. It avoids drying out, as well as being washed away, by clamping itself to the rocks with its powerful foot. Other mollusks do this as well. Sea hair, filamentous green algae, adds a splash of color.

THE UPPER INTERTIDAL ZONE

The upper intertidal remains exposed to the air except during high tides, when waves and currents wash over it. Rockweed is an indicator plant for this region.

The common acorn barnacle is still abundant in the upper part, but the channeled rock whelk and sometimes the frilled whelk, both snails common to the lower reaches of this zone, prey on it, significantly reducing its numbers. (The whelk's attack shelled creatures by drilling holes through their armor with a file-like structure called a radula.) Whelks also devour the thatched acorn barna-

Sitka periwinkles cluster together to feed on drift alga—a piece of kelp, which has been broken off and carried to shore by pounding waves.

ANNE WERTHEIM

ED COOPER

Gooseneck barnacles have rubbery stalks. The mussels beneath may eventually crowd them out. Storms clear way patches of mussels so that the goosenecks can grow in.

ANNE WERTHEIM

Lined chitons may be seen feeding on pink coralline algae in the lower intertidal zone.

ANNE WERTHEIM

Limpets are important intertidal grazers. They use a radula, a tongue like organ with horny teeth on it, to scrape algae off rocks.

cle, named for the thatched roof-like appearance of the sides of its shell. If it survives for a couple of years, however, its shell becomes so thick that the whelks cannot drill through it during the brief period the shell is submerged. The speckled limpet, the shield limpet, and the plate limpet are common in the upper intertidal. They also have radulas but they use them to graze on algae.

Some noteworthy algae include sea moss and sea lettuce. Sea palm takes over in patches created when strong surf rips away other plants and ani-mals. Sea tar, actually a seaweed, looks like a spot of tar on the rocks. Only recently, biologists realized that sea tar is another life stage of fleshy seaweed common in the next zone down.

Appearing in the tidepools are a number of unusual creatures. The hermit crab wears an empty snail shell for protection. As the crab grows, it discards its old home and moves into a new one. The tiny tidepool sculpin, characterized by its large head and goggle eyes, glides about the bottom of tidepools.

Sea palms depend on strong waves to clear away patches in mussel beds for growing space.

THE MIDDLE INTERTIDAL ZONE

The middle intertidal zone is covered and uncovered by salt water twice daily. Animals living here spend roughly half their time under water.

A striking feature of this zone is the band of mussels and gooseneck barnacles marking the upper limit. Two types of mussels live here: the edible or blue mussel, the smaller of the two, which lacks ribs on its shell; and the California mussel, which boasts longitudinal ribs. Both attach themselves to the rocks with fibrous strands called byssal threads. The edible mussel prefers quiet water because its byssal threads are not very strong. The California mussel thrives in the rough coastal water, however, forming dense clusters that provide homes for some three hundred kinds of small creatures.

The edible mussel may find protection from rough waves in a California mussel bed, but the sturdier California mussel can outgrow and crush its smaller neighbor. The edible mussel can easily crawl to the outside of a mussel community when new space is available.

Although larvae of the edible mussel seem to be less particular about selecting a site on which to settle, rough water does discourage them. California mussels prefer to settle among the byssal threads of their own kind as well as on sea moss, a small brushy seaweed.

Mixed in with the California mussels are gooseneck barnacles. They attach themselves with a tough, muscular stalk. They differ from other barnacles, not only in their shape, but also in the way they feed. While acorn barnacles actively beat their feathery antennae, called cirri, to gather food from the water, gooseneck barnacles simply spread their cirri and seine the water. Goosenecks apparently gain their foothold during the initial colonization of a bare rock or after strong waves, drifting logs and the like have cleared away the mussels. Goosenecks also grow on walls and under ledges, which mussels do not like. Although mussels can crowd out new goosenecks, wherever large numbers of goosenecks have become established, they are able to withstand the onslaught. And the goosenecks can fight back, for they fish with their cirri, eating the settling mussel larvae.

The sea palm also depend on rough waves and disturbances for survival; indeed, its presence is an indication of the rough conditions which create clearings in otherwise packed mussel beds. Sea palms, like goosenecks, grow on vertical walls or overhanging ledges. Algae common to higher areas, including sea moss and sea lettuce, persist in this zone. Sea cauliflower and sea sac, two small fleshy algae, appear here as well.

The upper distribution level of mussels is determined by the mussels' ability to withstand dryness. Mussels compete so well with other organisms that they effectively crowd out almost everything within their range.

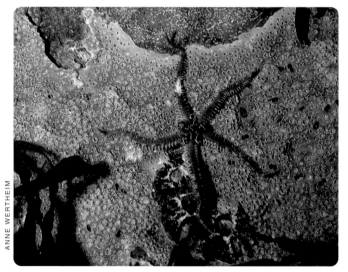

A brittlestar and pink hydrocoral add interest and color to the lower intertidal zone.

The ochre sea star preys heavily on mussels, affecting their lower limit of distribution. These mussels are heavily encrusted with barnacles.

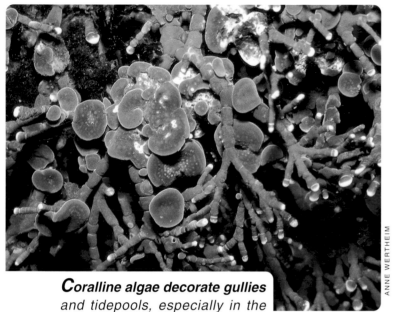

Coralline algae decorate gullies and tidepools, especially in the lower intertidal zone. Calcium carbonate, the hard material of teeth, bones, and seashells, makes them hard and gritty.

But in the midtidal zone, the ochre sea star prowls. Although it does eat other animals, it devours mussels so effectively that it defines their lower limit of growth throughout much of the coast. The sea star must feed under water, so its distribution is limited by the time available for feeding. Although the sea star can spend time out of water, it tends to stay close to the water to avoid drying out.

Some twenty-five species of organisms are dependent upon the sea star to keep mussels in check. Acorn barnacles, sea moss, and coralline algae become a lot more prevalent once the mussels are gone. Other, less noticeable seaweeds, including black pine and sea brush, become widespread as well. Sea cabbage is the dominant fleshy seaweed in the lower part of the middle intertidal.

The black chiton, which prefers to graze on sea cabbage, is also common. It has eight plates on its back, partially covered by a leathery girdle, and a muscular foot for clinging to rocks. By grazing on sea cabbage, the black chiton makes room for

The larger-spined red sea urchin and the purple sea urchin grow in the lower intertidal and subtidal zones. They feed mainly on drifting pieces of kelp and other algae.

Green sea anemones have stinging
cells on their tentacles, which they
use to stun their prey.

Although it prefers sand or mud, eelgrass may grow
in rocky tidepools washed by gentle waves.

coralline algae, which adds a dab of pink to rocks and tidepools. Whenever coralline algae are visible, grazing chitons or limpets usually have been at work.

Aggregating anemones, small animals with delicate pink to purple-tipped tentacles, find safety in numbers. Their tightly clustered colonies, spawned by cloning, decrease water loss during low tides, provide some protection from waves, and reduce the space available to competing organisms. When one colony encounters another, its members engage in border warfare to protect their territory.

THE LOWER INTERTIDAL ZONE

The lower intertidal zone benefits from a protective layer of seawater during all but the lowest of tides. Here life flourishes, continuing into the subtidal zone, where an even greater variety, abundance, and explosion of bright colors are found.

Split kelp and purple sea urchins are indicators of the lower intertidal. Bull kelp also appears, tossed ashore in twisted tangles ripped loose from subtidal beds. Also growing offshore are beds of feather boa, giant, and Alaria kelp. Pterygophora flourishes in the shallow subtidal and often washes ashore as well.

A wide variety of other seaweeds is present, including Turkish towel, a well-named plant; red

laver, whose thin rubbery blades reflect a full spectrum of colors; and the rainbow seaweed, whose thick multicolored blades appear oily. Several less conspicuous seaweeds whose common names hint at their fascinating shapes include the red eyelet silk, the cup and saucer, and the sea staghorn. Over a dozen small species of pink coralline algae grow in tidepools. The list goes on and on.

Sea stars increase. The ochre sea star uses this region as a refuge. The mottled sea star comes in many colors, with thin gangly arms and a splotchy appearance. The six-rayed or brooding sea star is a delight to watch as it carefully tends its tiny but perfectly shaped offspring. The blood star, appropriately enough, is bright orange or red. The pink and the vermilion sea stars are equally well named. The sunflower, sun star, and rose star all sport elaborate designs of blues, purples, tans, pinks, and other shades. Three sea urchins, the green, the red, and the purple, brighten this region as well.

Sea urchins, like many other intertidal animals, lay eggs that develop into planktonic larvae. Their young spend considerable time drifting at the mercy of the currents before settling into a favorable habitat. The success of the sea urchin larvae in colonizing a shore seems to depend on a widespread invasion of larvae throughout the coast of North America. This occurs only every few years.

The stems of split kelp develop growth rings similar to those of trees. These rings reflect seasonal cycles and can be used to age the plant.

The variety of crab increases in the lower intertidal, as well as their shape, color, and behavior. The decorator, the sharp-nosed, and the helmet crabs are camouflaged with bits of seaweed, small colonizing animals, and other organisms. The hairy crab deserves its name, and the umbrella or turtle crab, whose upper shell covers its body, is one of the most unusual ones of all. Hermit crabs also inhabit this region.

Mollusks take on character and variety. The purple-hinged rock scallop cements one of its shells to the bottom and a collection of other creatures often grow upon it. The piddock bores into solid rock, and the leafy hornmouth, with its three winged ridges, not only preys on barnacles and other snails, but also drills through rocks to feed on piddocks.

Other chitons join the black one. Mossy and hairy chitons sport bristles on their girdles. The lined chiton has a beautiful pattern of colors running across its plates. The giant chiton, which can reach a length of nearly a foot, lives here, its plates covered by a reddish brown gritty hide. Limpets from higher zones are joined by the keyhole limpet, which has a hole in the top of its shell, and the dunce cap limpet, which feeds on pink coralline algae.

The giant green sea anemone obtains its bright color from microscopic green algae, which supplies nutrition to the animal. Just as trees penetrate other zones because of the effects of river valleys, green anemones also grow into the washes and gullies of the middle intertidal. The red and green anemone has a light gray shank streaked with red. The unusual brooding anemone, like the brooding sea star, derives its name from keeping its young close by. The tiny creatures surrounding the parents are quite a sight. On rare occasions, the stately column and tentacles of the white-plumed anemone may be seen here too.

Sophisticated interrelationships exist between animals of the lower intertidal. Black chitons, limpets, and other grazers feed on seaweeds, creating space for coralline algae to grow. Without these grazers, the coralline algae would be crowded out by the larger seaweeds. But the lined chiton and the dunce cap limpet depend on coralline algae for food. Thus if the black chiton is removed from the scene, a domino effect will occur, ultimately resulting in a decrease in the lined chiton population.

In the intertidal and subtidal, where sea urchins live, a similar relationship exists. Sea gulls and sunflower stars prey on the urchins, while offshore, a moderate population of sea otters also eats urchins, which in turn graze on kelp. Without these predators, the sea urchins could wipe out the kelp beds. Kelp beds have a moderating effect on waves that impact the shore. They also serve as a good habitat for many kinds of fish.

The intertidal zone is an ideal place to study nature because the patterns of life are compressed into such small spaces. The display of color and form in this region is magnificent, but people should look, not touch. When disturbed, the creatures soon disappear or retreat to the subtidal area. Unfortunately, intertidal life along much of the Pacific coast has been drastically depleted because of a few thoughtless people.

The seashore is more than a narrow strip where the land meets the sea, though; it is also the migration path for many creatures. Steelhead trout and five species of salmon swim across river

Gulls rest peacefully on the roots of a huge driftwood log.

mouths to travel upstream and breed. The surf smelt actually breed on the beaches in the park, while migrating whales spout just offshore. The gray is by far the most common, but humpback, little piked, finback, blue, sei, and sperm whales also pass by farther offshore. Northern fur seals, elephant seals, and California sea lions roam along the coast, while Steller sea lions and harbor seals are natives to this region. Sea otters are occasionally seen offshore, along with the more common river otter, which is usually seen in streams or on beaches.

Deer, elk, raccoons, and bear wander along the shore. Mink regularly raid the beaches for sea urchins, crabs, and other shellfish, as well as for the eggs of gulls and oystercatchers.

The offshore islands, which are jointly managed by the National Park Service, the U.S. Fish and Wildlife Service, and the Olympic Coast National Marine Sanctuary, are preserves for sea birds. The pelagic cormorant, common murre, rhinoceros auklet, and pigeon guillemot are but a few that visit the coast. The black oystercatcher preys on shellfish, but it is very sensitive to human disturbance. Thus it serves as one of the indicators of the health of the seashore community. Hopefully, its distinctive call and antics will bring enjoyment to visitors forever.

SUGGESTED READING

CAREFOOT, THOMAS. *Pacific Seashores: A Guide to Intertidal Ecology.* Seattle: University of Washington Press, 1977.

KOZLOFF, EUGENE N. *Seashore Life of the Northern Pacific Coast.* Seattle: University of Washington Press, 1983.

SNIVELY, GLORIA. *Exploring the Seashore in British Columbia, Washington and Oregon.* Ventura, California: Western Marine Enterprises, Inc., 1979.

WERTHEIM, ANNE. *The Intertidal Wilderness.* Anne Wertheim, 1984.

In 1778 Captain James Cook became the first English navigator to explore the Pacific Northwest.

Before There Was a Park

American Indians have lived on the Olympic Peninsula for at least twelve thousand years. After the continental ice sheets retreated, but before the great forests started, bison, caribou and elephants roamed the peninsula. From a discovery at the Manis mastodon site at Sequim we believe that man fed on these ancient elephants.

Other evidence of early habitation comes from a twenty-five-hundred-year-old fishing site near the Hoko River mouth at the Strait of Juan de Fuca. Indians, apparently in canoes, fished the strait for halibut and other bottom fish.

But the clearest window into the past comes

Mountaineering skills are required to ascend Mount Olympus. Parties should consist of three or more persons.

from the site of the Ozette Village, where mud-flows entombed cultural artifacts in much the same way that volcanic ash preserved Pompeii. The beautiful Makah Cultural and Research Center in Neah Bay displays a wealth of material recovered from this site.

A COMPLEX CULTURE EMERGES

The two-thousand-year-old Makah culture was very elaborate. The Indians had a strong economy based on a plentiful supply of natural resources. They carved dugout canoes, some up to thirty feet long, out of western red cedar logs, using them to hunt whales, seals, sea lions, and sea otters. They also used them in warfare. They built communal longhouses, about thirty-five feet wide and seventy feet long, from red cedar planks. Whale bones were used to construct drainage systems. Elaborately carved fish clubs, spears, bowls, boxes, adzes, chisels, and knives were common. Hand spindles and vertical looms were used in transforming dog wool into blankets. Cedar bark was woven into robes, capes, skirts, aprons, and mats. Cedar and other materials were made into baskets.

TOM MYERS

Dugout canoes were important to the Indian economy. They were used in fishing, in hunting marine mammal, in warfare, and for transportation. About thirty feet long, they were hollowed out of red cedar logs. Steam was used to soften the sides so they could be flared. Such canoes are occasionally used today, although outboard motors sometimes replace traditional paddles.

TOM MYERS

Indians on the peninsula have traditionally worked with only native materials like cedar bark, mammal skins, antlers, bones, and shells. Today, glass beads are used in some Indian work.

DAVE HUNTZINGER

Food was plentiful. Salmon swarmed upstream. Smelt were dipped from the surf, and crab and mussels abounded on beaches. Indians scraped barnacles off the rocks to eat, and women sometimes cooked limpets on the spot by covering them with seaweed and hot rocks. Elk, deer, and birds provided meat. Roots and berries in season supplemented their diet. Food gathering was largely seasonal, concentrated during a three- or four-month period, which permitted much winter leisure time.

A sophisticated social system evolved from this leisure and wealth. Longhouses and canoes in each village were owned in common, but the inheritance and possession of other material goods divided the society into the privileged and the commoners. Power and prestige were based on ostentatious displays of wealth in the form of great feasts and in the ownership of slaves, usually women and children captured during battles. Many slaves were ransomed, but some were doomed to lives of servitude. Treated as mere property, they might be given away as gifts along with other goods during a feast, or potlatch.

A potlatch usually celebrated a special event, such as the birth of an heir, the marriage of an important person, or the ransoming of a slave. Guests were invited from many tribes and might number in the hundreds. Gifts usually were given to other wealthy individuals who were obligated to give larger gifts in return at a later potlatch. The act of giving served to elevate an Indian's social position and to strengthen tribal ties.

When white explorers reached this region in the 1770's, perhaps nine thousand Indians were distributed in nine major groups and four smaller bands living in many small villages along the coastal lowlands.

Today, fishing, timber, and tourism play key roles in the economy of Indian tribes. Sophisticated modern technology has replaced many past practices, but a strong sense of identity and pride in traditional values continue to play important roles in the Indian way of life on the peninsula.

THE EXPLORERS AND SETTLERS

The first European explorers came by sea in search of the Northwest Passage, which supposedly crossed the New World leading to the riches of the East. Possibly the first European to sight the Olympic Peninsula was Aspostlos Valerianos, a Greek pilot who sailed for Spain under the name of Juan de Fuca. He claimed to have sailed into the

Sol Duc Falls hints at some of the wonders that had been rumored to exist in the heart of the Olympics. But dense vegetation made travel inland difficult—one of the reasons why the Olympics remained unexplored by white men for so long.

DAVID MUENCH

Marymere Falls and many other attractions require only moderate effort to get there.

a high profit. News of Captain Cook's fortunes soon brought a flood of English and Americans to the Pacific coast.

In 1787, Charles Barclay, whose seventeen-year-old bride was the first white woman to visit the area, named the Strait of Juan de Fuca. The following year, Captain John Meares, an English trader, gave Mount Olympus its name. It seemed to be a good place for the home of the mythical Greek gods.

In 1790, the Spanish explorer Alférez Manuel Quimper charted the shores of the strait. The following year, Juan Francisco de Eliza, a Spanish sea captain, named Port Angeles. The Spaniards established a military post a year later at Neah Bay, consisting of more than ten houses. This small colony, which lasted only five months, was the first attempt by Europeans to settle on the peninsula. During this period, Captain Robert Gray, an American, discovered a harbor at the southern end of the peninsula, which bears his name today. Also in the same year, Captain George Vancouver explored Puget Sound in search of the Northwest Passage. He named Port Townsend and Discovery Bay and strengthened England's claim to the Pacific Northwest.The determined British won the land from the Spanish, only to give way to the Americans and their Manifest Destiny. Finally, in 1846, the forty-ninth parallel was established as the boundary between American and British territory west of the Rockies.

In 1851, Port Townsend became the first permanent western settlement on the peninsula, but the rugged interior attracted little attention. The first cross-mountain trip appears to have occurred in September 1878, when Melbourne Watkinson, Benjamin and Charles Armstrong, George McLaughlin, and Finley McCrae journeyed from the Hood Canal over the southern Olympics to the mouth of the Quinault River on the coast. The route of their eleven-day trip is uncertain, but they may have climbed Mount Olson or Mount Duckabush. They did not map the area and their trip apparently went unnoticed by later explorers.

In 1885, Lieutenant Joseph P. O'Neil led six men in the first systematic attempt by Westerners to explore the interior. They laboriously cut a mule trail, which today is approximated by the park road to Hurricane Ridge. Their trail continued to Obstruction Point down into Grand and Cameron

strait that bears his name in 1592, but satisfactory proof of his voyage is decidedly lacking.

The first well-documented voyage was by Juan Perez Hernandez, claiming territory for the Spanish Crown. On August 11, 1774, he sailed past Mount Olympus and named it Santa Rosalia. The following year, Bruce de Heceta, commanding the Spanish ship, Santiago, went ashore at Point Grensville, near the Quinault River, to plant a cross and take formal possession of the land for Spain. But close by, several men from a sister ship, the Sonora, were killed during an encounter with three hundred Indians near the Island of Sorrows, now Destruction Island.

In 1778, Captain James Cook became the first English navigator to explore the Pacific Northwest. He named Cape Flattery, but failed to find the Strait of Juan de Fuca. He sailed on to China, where he sold sea otter furs from the Northwest at

The major challenge facing the staff of Olympic National Park is to allow visitors to enjoy beautiful places like Lake Angeles, while still protecting the resources for future generations. Fortunately, visitors are becoming increasingly conscientious users of such resources.

basins. From here, O'Neil and his sidekick, Private John Johnson, scouted on foot up the slopes of Mount Anderson. The project was interrupted when O'Neil was transferred, but he had penetrated the heart of the region and paved the way for future explorations.

Stories of Sir Henry Stanley's adventures in Africa, sponsored by newspapers in New York and London, filled the air, so The Seattle Times sponsored an expedition into the Olympics. One tale claimed a charmed paradise lay hidden in the mountains; another, a tribe of cannibals.

The Press expedition, led by James H. Christie, left Port Angeles in December 1889, and emerged five and a half months later at Lake Quinault. The hardships, privations, and dangers they overcame that winter would have destroyed less hardy and spirited men. They pushed their way up the Elwha River, the Goldie River, along the ridge leading to Mount Wilder, down into the Elwha Valley again, over Low Divide, and down to

It took the Press Expedition nearly six months to cross the Olympics in 1889. Today that same trip normally takes four to five days.

ED COOPER

Mountain Climbing

Two white men and two Indians reportedly climbed Mount Olympus in 1854, but there is no documentation of this event. In 1890 James Bretherton climbed one of the lesser peaks of Mount Olympus, probably in the Hoh Glacier cirque. The first verified climb on Mount Olympus occurred in 1899, when Jack McGlone climbed it alone and left a record of his climb in a tin box on East Peak. Hershell C. Parker, Belmore H. Browne, and Walter G. Clarke climbed Middle Peak on July 17, 1907, mistaking it for the highest peak. On August 12 of the same year, a group from the Mountaineers Club climbed East Peak and found McGlone's tin box. The next day, I. A. Nelson and ten others climbed Middle Peak and found a cairn left by Parker, Browne, and Clarke, then climbed West Peak, the highest of the three at 7,980 feet.

Why climb a mountain? According to George Mallory, a famous mountain climber, "Because it's there."

"Because it's there"

-GEORGE MALLORY

Temperature changes can be rapid and extreme on Mount Olympus. Sunburn and freezing can be threats on the same trip.

ED COOPER

A climber approaches Middle Peak on Mount Olympus. Three peaks form the crown of Mount Olympus and eight glaciers radiate from its summit.

The two climbers to the right of the peak look like ants on the slopes of Mount Olympus. Life's daily problems pale into insignificance during such adventures.

Crevasses a hundred or more feet deep form as glaciers flow down steep slopes.

-59-

People can still walk in coastal forests which look the way they were before the white man came. The park is a vignette of primitive America.

Lake Quinault. They blazed a trail across the Olympics, which can now be traversed not 1/3 in four or five days. The Bailey Range is named after the newspaper owner who sponsored the expedition. Mount Christie and Mount Barnes honor the leader and narrator of the expedition.

In July 1890, Lieutenant O'Neil returned to lead a fifteen-man expedition from Port Union, on the Hood Canal, across the mountains to Lake Quinault. The Oregon Alpine Club provided three staff scientists and much of the funding. The expedition punched a mule trail up the north fork of the Skokomish River, over O'Neil Pass, down Enchanted Valley, and out the east fork of the Quinault. O'Neil Pass, Creek, and Peak are named for the Lieutenant; Mount Henderson for the botanist; and Mount Bretherton after the naturalist and cartographer.

O'Neil was the first to advocate a national park on the Olympic Peninsula. Ironically, he had to assert the Olympics were "absolutely unfit for any use, except perhaps as a national park where elk and deer can be saved," as part of his argument.

In 1897, President Cleveland created the Olympic Forest Reserve to prevent the great forests of the peninsula from being destroyed by poor logging practices. After the turn of the century, several bills were introduced to protect the wildlife, particularly the elk, on the peninsula, but none passed.

Finally, in 1909, President Theodore Roosevelt proclaimed the area a national monument. In 1938, President Franklin D. Roosevelt signed a bill establishing Olympic National Park. Later, more area was added to the park, until over 1,400 square miles lay within its boundaries. In 1988, more than 865,000 acres, which is 95 percent of the park land, were set aside as a formal wilderness.

SUGGESTED READING

BERGLAND, ERIC O., AND JERRY MARR. *Prehistoric Life on the Olympic Peninsula.* Seattle: Pacific Northwest National Parks and Forests Association, 1988.
WOOD, ROBERT L. *Across the Olympic Mountains.* Seattle: The Mountaineers, 1989.

SUGGESTED DVD

Olympic National Park, DVD #DV-98, 62 minutes, Whittier, California: Finley-Holiday Films.

Carved by a glacier, Lake Crescent originally flowed toward the east. Later, a rock avalanche divided it into Crescent and Sutherland lakes, and it now drains to the north. An Indian legend alleges that Mount Storm King became angry because the Quileute and Klallam Indians were fighting, so he threw down a rock, forming the two lakes.

All About Olympic National Park

Discover Your Northwest

The DYNW is a non-profit organization which supports educational and informational programs at Olympic and other northwest national parks and forests. Through the sale of books and other interpretive items, the association funds the production of park trail guides, visitor information newspapers, visitor center exhibits, and special projects that enhance visitor services. The DYNW contributed to their production of a major primeval forest exhibit and children's discovery room, both located in the park's main visitor center. The park's Junior Ranger program, sponsoring summer activities for young visitors, is also funded by the association.

For information about the park:

Write to
Olympic National Park
600 E. Park Avenue
Port Angeles, WA
98362-6798

Park information #
(360)565-3130

Fax #
(360)565-3015

Website:
www.nps.gov/olym

Pileated woodpecker
PERRY D. SLOCUM / ANIMALS ANIMALS

Olympic National Park
Junior Ranger

Why is it so important to preserve Olympic National Park? Are you aged 5 or above? Start an adventure today by traveling the web of life through Olympic National Park.

Obtain your Junior Ranger Booklet from the visitor center and begin your adventure through the park - any direction will do... Play a game of Nature Hike Bingo as you hike the trails, become a Seashore Detective, join a ranger for a walk into Olympics wilderness, or attend an evening campfire program.

In the winter join a park ranger on a snowshow walk. Learning about the importance of having this park and many more throughout the country can be fun and exciting. It is up to you! Once your day has come to an end and you have completed the activities, tell a ranger and recite the Junior Ranger Pledge, you will then receive a Junior Ranger certificate and badge – wear it with pride.

Come visit again and start the adventure all over again!

OLYMPIC NATIONAL PARK

DUNGENESS NATIONAL
WILDLIFE REFUGE

Old
Town

DUNGENESS
RECREATION AREA

Dungeness

Agnew

Salt Creek

Lyre River

Joyce

112

112

Angeles
Point

LOWER ELWHA KLALLAM
INDIAN RESERVATION

EDIZ HOOK

PORT ANGELES

101

Park
Headquarters

Olympic National Park
Visitor Center

Sequim

101

Kitchen-Dick Road

Log Cabin
Resort

East Beach

101

Fairholme

North Shore

LAKE CRESCENT

Storm King
Information Station

Heart O' the Hills

Mount Pleasant

Buck Knoll

THE FOOTHILLS

La Poel

Lake Crescent
Lodge

Aurora Peak

Mount Storm King

Mount Baldy

Altair

Elwha

Lizard Head
Peak

LAKE RIDGE

Little River Trail

Mt Angeles

Dungeness
Forks

HURRICANE RIDGE

Eagle

Sol Duc Hot
Springs Resort

Boulder Peak

Slide Pass

Slide Pk

Appleton Pass

SEVEN LAKES BASIN

Whiskey Bend
Krause Bottom
Humes Ranch

Hurricane
Ridge
Visitor Center

Eagle Point

Elk Mountain

Slab Camp

Blue
Mountain

Cliff
Camp

Twomile
Camp

Camp Tony

Slide Camp

Bogachiel Peak

Green Peak

HIGH DIVIDE

Cat Peak

Mt Carrie

MOUNT
FITZHENRY

Obstruction Peak

Deer Park

Tyler Peak

Baldy

arloaf Mountain

Dodger Pt

BAILE RANGE

Olympus

World's largest
subalpine fir

Elkhorn

Grand Pass

GRAY WOLF RIDGE

Camp
Handy

Hoh Rain Forest
Visitor Center

Mt Scott

Cameron
Pass

Mt Deception

Mt Fricaba

Boulder

Glacier Meadows

Hayes River

Mt Claywood

Mt Mystery

MOUNT OLYMPUS
West Pk
7980 ft.
Middle Pk
7930 ft.

East Peak
7780 ft.

Mt Barnes

Mt Dana

Wellesley Pk

Sentinel Peak

South Fork

Mt Wilder

Sentinels
Sister

DIAMOND MOUNTAIN

Dosewallips

Elkhorn

Mt Anderson

The Brothers

Low Divide

Mt Christie

World's largest
western hemlock

La Crosse Pass

Skyline Ridge Trail

Enchanted Valley

Lena Lake Camp

Mt Bretherton

Park's largest
Douglas-fir

O'Neil Pass

O'Neil Peak

Lena Creek

Hamma Hamma

OLYMPIC

Park's largest
yellow cedar

North Fork

Mt Olson

Mt Olson

NATIONAL

OLYMPIC

Graves Creek

NATIONAL

FOREST

FOREST

Quinault
Rain Forest

July Creek

LAKE QUINAULT

Falls Creek

North Shore Road

South Shore Road

Camp
Harps

Wynoochee Falls

Staircase

LAKE CUSHMAN

LAKE CUSHMAN
STATE PARK

A Look to the Future

Some view Olympic as three great parks in one: the temperate rain forest, the high mountains, and the splendid coast. Others prize it as the greatest remaining vignette of primitive America in the contiguous forty-eight states.

Scientists consider Olympic a storehouse of genetic diversity which protects us against future catastrophes, since America today depends on relatively few genetic strains of plants for food and fiber. At Olympic National Park, plants and animals obey nature's laws with scant interference by man. The park thereby serves as a scientific control for measuring the effects of utilizing natural resources in other areas.

ED COOPER

Most of all, the park is a place for people to enjoy. Adventure awaits those who seek it; so does solitude in still, quiet places. Each bend in a road or trail beckons us to new scenes that tease our eyes. Nature's perfumes and melodies delight and refresh us. Her many facets can be studied with the deadly earnestness of a scientist—or just for the fun of it.

In Olympic we can be awed by nature's grandeur, enjoy healthy outdoor recreation, or be touched by history. Olympic National Park is truly a special place of immeasurable value.

KC Publications has been the leading publisher of colorful, interpretive books about National Park areas, public lands, Indian Culture, and related subjects for over 45 years. We have 5 active series – over 125 titles – with Translation Packages in up to 8 languages for over half the areas we cover.   Write, call, or visit our web site for our full-color catalog.

Our series are:

The Story Behind the Scenery® – Compelling stories of over 65 National Park areas and similar Public Land areas. Some with Translation Packages.

in pictures... Nature's Continuing Story® – A companion, pictorially oriented, series on America's National Parks.   All titles have Translation Packages.

For Young Adventurers® – Dedicated to young seekers and keepers of all things wild and sacred. Explore America's Heritage from A to Z.

Voyage of Discovery® – Exploration of the expansion of the western United States.

Indian Culture and the Southwest – All about Native Americans, past and present.

To receive our full-color catalog featuring:
    Over 125 titles – Books and other related specialty products.
Call (800) 626-9673, Fax (928) 684-5189, Write to the address below,
    Or visit our web site at www.nationalparksbooks.com

Published by KC Publications • P.O. Box 3615 • Wickenburg, AZ 85358

Inside back cover: Captain John Meares named this Mount Olympus in 1788—as befitting the Greek gods. Photo by D.C. Lowe/Aperture

Back cover: The temperate rain forest of Olympic is one of the world's greatest treasures. Photo by David Muench

Created, Designed, and Published in the U.S.A.
Printed by Tien Wah Press (Pte.) Ltd, Singapore
Pre-Press by United Graphic Pte. Ltd